I Robert Pattinson

Harlee Harte

DOVE
B O O K S

I ♥ Robert Pattinson

The opinions expressed in this book are those of the author of this book and do not necessarily reflect the views of the publisher or its affiliates.

ISBN-10: 1-59777-649-1
ISBN-13: 978-1-59777-649-3
Library of Congress Cataloging-In-Publication Data Available

Cover & Book Design by Sonia Fiore

Printed in the United States of America

Dove Books, Inc.
9465 Wilshire Boulevard, Suite 840
Beverly Hills, CA 90212

10 9 8 7 6 5 4 3 2 1

Collect all four
Harlee Harte books

I ♡ Taylor Swift

I ♡ The Jonas Brothers

I ♡ Selena Gomez

I ♡ Robert Pattinson

Hi!

I'm Harlee Harte.

I write the celebrity column, "HarteBeat," for the Hollywoodland High School newspaper. It's a blast! I get to meet and greet the hottest teen idols and hit the hip Tinseltown places to hang out and shop while I'm on the hunt. Being a columnist is hard work, but I just love the glamour and excitement! I'm always looking for the latest news about our favorite stars, so visit my Facebook page and see what I have going on or just say hello. My friends Kiki, Marcy, and Luzie pop in every now and then, too, and love to chime in on the latest fashions, cool beauty tips, music, celeb sightings, and advice on how to deal with parents, school, crushes, and friends.

I'd love to hear from you!

Harlee Harte

TABLE OF CONTENTS

PART ONE
The Assignment

"Omigod," I shrieked. "Could this day get any worse?" You'd think that Harlee Harte, celebrity reporter for the *Hollywoodland Star*, with her own press pass, thank you very much, would lead a charmed life. But no. Not even close. First, I woke up with a pimple on my nose, second I got a B in history, on a test I actually studied for, and then at lunch who did I have to sit next to but the utterly annoying Philip Pendleton IV. He pestered me all through lunch, insisting that he needs my celebrity column a day early this week because he has to fly out to Boston for something to do with Harvard. Like I care. And I have no idea who to write my column on because every time I sit down to write something an image of my crush, the gorgeous Jack Kelly, floats into my head, and I compose long paragraph after paragraph about his blue eyes, his mischievous grin, the slight huskiness to his voice. And then, to make things even worse, when I arrived home from school I found out some really bad news.

"What d'you mean I have to babysit Alec?" I whined. "You know I can't do that. It's inhumane of you to ask."

My mom rolled her eyes. "I have to go to a meeting, and I can't bring him with me. Just play *Mutant Weasels from Mars* or one of his other favorite games, and you'll be fine. I mean, Harlee, is it really too much to ask of you to spend time with your adorable little brother?"

I looked at my mom to see if she was being serious. She was, and then she was gone. Immediately I jumped into action and texted Luzie.

Me: omg I need ur help!!!!!!
Luzie: sup? I hv a soccer game...
wont b home til 10
Me: hv 2 babysit Alec LLL ughhhhh
Luzie: sry! G2g ttyl

Great. Just my luck. Luzie's always amazing with Alec. She has little brothers of her own and loads of cousins. I should have known that she'd have a soccer game, though, as she plays like five times a week.

From upstairs, I heard, "Harlee! I'm bored. Come play with me!" My heart dropped even further. Maybe Marcy could come over and help entertain pesky little Alec.

Me: plz come over nowwwww
Marcy: noooo wayyyy. @ poetry club

Which sounds really nerdy, but Marcy is great with words and thinks she might be a singer-songwriter one day. Of course, there's a really cute boy who goes there too, kind of Goth-looking, kind of skater-boy. And that made me think about my own Jack Kelly again. I wondered if he likes me. Well, I knew he did, but I wanted him not to like me as a friend. *As a girlfriend*. My happy thoughts were interrupted by Alec's shout from his bedroom.

"Harlee, mom said you have to play with me. I'm gonna tell her you ignored me and were on your phone the whole time, and she'll take it away from you. She'll con-fis-cate it," he added gleefully. It's a word he hears a lot in this house, especially about my phone. I headed up the stairs, infuriated, and stuck my head around his door. "Wanna play *Escape from the Dementors* or *Dumbledore's Army*?'" he asked, as if it was super kind of him to give me a choice.

"Neither," I said. "We're going out." I had a plan. I would babysit—but on my terms. I wasn't going to stay home and play video games with my little bro like I didn't have a life.

"Let's go," I said.

"Where?" asked Alec, getting ready to fight.

"For candy. And to Jamba Juice. And maybe to see Kiki."

If Alec weren't just eight years old, I would say he had a major crush on my friend, Kiki. She is great, even hot, but…

"OK," he said, much faster than expected. "Lots of candy."

Later...

I love Robertson Boulevard, and it felt good to be there, even with Alec. He wasn't being too much of a pain, slurping his second smoothie which meant no talking from him. I was hoping to run into Kiki, practicing her favorite sport, shopping, and then the afternoon could even go under the category of "fun."

I was just thinking this, and wondering whether I could afford to buy any new clothes, when I caught sight of a group of kids from school across the street. Sondra, that girl who thinks she's so great from the newspaper, Toby (are they an item?) looking pretty good in a DC hoodie, Luzie's boyfriend Joey, and Jack. Jack? My heart missed a beat. No way I could be seen here with my kid brother, more-to-the-point my loud-mouthed kid brother who knows I have a crush on Jack.

"This way," I hissed at Alec, grabbing hold of his arm and tugging him along. Why, oh why, was I wearing platform sandals and a skirt that suddenly seemed too tight? I looked back. Oh no, they were crossing over. Had they seen me or were they just heading to Jamba Juice? Was that someone yelling my name? I stumbled around the corner down an alley, still dragging Alec with me, so that he was side-skipping, his mouth suctioned onto his straw, making outraged gurgling noises. We swung onto Third Street, away from the crowds, and finally I released my grip.

"In here," I gasped at him and shoved him into a small, dark bakery. "We should be safe." I sounded like Kiki who is always being extra-cautious about where we meet, what she says. I guess you just never know who might be listening in Hollywood, and which Web site it might end up on.

"Are we being chased by police, or Martians?" asked Alec looking at me with what had to be described as awe. I had inspired awe in my little brother. Maybe he was adorable.

"I want one of those," he said, pointing at some cream-filled puff concoction which he knew would cost me half my allowance and that mom would never allow him to eat. Forget I said adorable. I handed over a huge sum of money for the sugar bomb and slunk into the only booth with Alec, sliding low down in the old leather seat, keeping my eyes on the door.

Across from us, some guy in a hoodie opened up a diet Coke. I looked briefly at him then turned my attention back to the door. Alex stuffed his face with cream. Gross. I pretended he wasn't with me.

"That looks good," said the guy in the hoodie in a surprisingly deep voice with a cute British accent.

"It is. D'you want some?" To my horror, Alec broke off a smushy piece and handed it to the guy who grinned. "No, thanks, I wouldn't deprive you."

"OK. I'm Alec, by the way. You were in Harry Potter, weren't you?"

Oh great, so Alec thinks he's talking to a dementor or something. I rolled my eyes and started to text Kiki.

"Yeah, that's right. People don't usually remember that though. Not now. I must say, it's pretty refreshing to not have people call me…"

I looked up. "Edward!" I shrieked!

He turned to me in horror, his blue-grey eyes wide, pulled up his hood, and slunk down in the seat. "Not so loud," he whispered. "Unless you want to get mobbed. Which I don't recommend."

He didn't have to worry. I was speechless. My tongue had turned to jelly in my mouth. I couldn't have spoken even if winged Martians had flown into the bakery and swooped off with Alec. I was sitting across from Robert Pattinson—completely gorgeous, totally crush-worthy Robert Pattinson, star of my favorite movie in the world. I could reach out and touch him. Wait until I told Kiki, Luzie, and Marcy about this.

"I was just saying it's nice not to be called Edward all the time. Anyway, who are you hiding from?" he asked me. Robert Pattinson addressed a question to me. My mouth opened but no sound came out. "Some boys," said Alec. "Someone she has a crush on. Like Jack." He grinned, all pleased with himself.

I stared at him in amazement. He knew?! I thought he was just a dumb eight-year-old.

"Girls," said Robert Pattinson, shaking his head. "They're so complicated." Then he and Alec laughed like they were accomplices. "Especially my sister," added Alec. That annoyed me enough for my voice to come back.

"Hi, I'm Harlee. And I'm not that complicated. Just enough to be interesting but not too much to be weird."

He smiled at me. "It must be nice to be interesting. I'm pretty boring myself. Oh no." He ducked down in his seat. "Someone must have spotted me. Soon I'll have a pack of girls screaming at me. Can you help get me out of here?"

I nodded, all-action suddenly, a highly trained professional once more. Quickly I explained the situation to the old lady behind the counter, and she looked dreamily at Robert, as if he were her favorite grandson or something. She beckoned us through a side door into the kitchen, which smelled delicious, then showed us a back door. "This is good," she whispered. "You come back any time you want," she said looking at Robert. He grinned. "Thanks."

We sneaked out into the alley and then cut across to Alden Street. "Try and look normal," said Robert, and I realized how tall he was now that he was standing up. And hunky. "They won't be expecting me to be with anyone. May I? Just to the end of the street? I can find my own way to the Sofitel from there," and he put an arm around my shoulders, took hold of Alec's hand, and we set off down the street, like any other couple and the kid brother. "Are you sure you don't mind?" he asked. I shook my head. Why would I mind? It felt very nice to be snuggled under his arm. He started telling a funny story about his older sisters, just to talk and be natural so we didn't draw attention. And we didn't. I told him I'm Harlee Harte, celebrity reporter for the *Hollywoodland Star*, and asked if I could take his photo and interview him. But before he could answer someone shouted my name. *Toby*. I've known his voice since Kindergarten.

I turned and saw him across the street with Sondra and Joey and Jack. They were all staring at me. And Jack seemed to be staring most of all.

"Oh, hi," I shouted, as if it were the most natural thing in the world for me to be out strolling with some hunk wrapped around me. "This is—" and I stopped. I could feel my cheeks burning. "This is Alec," I muttered, and then we left. We kept on walking. Robert said, "I'm really sorry. That was awkward. I'm so sorry." He sounded genuinely apologetic and looked sad. "It's OK, it'll be fine," I managed to say but inside I felt sick. My stomach was churning. I kept thinking about the look on Jack's face.

At the end of the street we parted ways. "Thank you, Harlee Harte and Alec," Robert said. He turned to walk away then stopped, "I'd be grateful if you kept the name of my hotel secret."

The next day...

The next morning I overslept and got to school just as the late bell was ringing. I rushed over to my locker to cram my books inside.

"Where were you?" asked Marcy. "Even Kiki got here before you. What's up? You don't look good."

I didn't feel good. I had walked past Jack Kelly over by his locker, and his back was turned directly towards me, but I thought he saw me. Did he ignore me? Was I imagining it? Then I saw Kiki and Luzie striding purposely towards me. Luzie was not smiling, probably the first time ever I had seen that. And her iPod headphones were not jammed into her ears. And from the other side of the hallway Philip Pendleton IV was trotting towards me, eyes all eager beneath their wire frames. I felt like I was in one of Alec's crazy video games. How could I escape?

They all converged on me at the same time. Kiki asked, "Who's the guy?" while Luzie said, "Why didn't you tell us?" Then they stood there, all attitude, hands on their hips, like BFFs betrayed. Marcy looked confused. I was glad when I was able to turn to Philip Pendleton IV who rapped out a question, "I'm expecting your column. Tomorrow, 4th period?"

"Yeah, yeah, I know, or you'll give it to Sondra to write. You'll have it. I'm writing it on Robert Pattinson."

For a moment Kiki, Luzie, and Marcy forgot they were mad at me and all gushed "Edward Cullen," "He's in town to promote his new movie." "Apparently," added Marcy.

I took this opportunity to escape into class.

At lunch time, though, they were waiting for me at our table. I walked straight to them through the crowded lunchroom, not wanting to make eye contact with anyone, not wanting to look at Jack Kelly and have him look away and ignore me. But try as I might I did see him. His back was towards me again. And was that Sondra at his table? I clenched my teeth and walked by, head held high.

"OK," said Marcy, not even giving me a chance to sit down. "We want to know everything."

I shrugged. I had thought it would be fun to tell them about Robert but now it had all turned awkward.

"Joey told me you were on Third Street with some tall guy yesterday…that you looked like you were really into him. We thought you liked Jack. What's going on?"

"I do. And there's nothing going on." Then I launched into my whole story: babysitting, shopping, looking for Kiki, seeing Jack and not wanting to bump into him with Alec. And then the Robert Pattinson part of the story.

As I told them everything that had happened their mouths hung open, and Luzie even grinned again.

"No way," shouted Kiki, and high-fived me, drawing way more attention to our table than I was comfortable with.

"And he put his arm around you?" Luzie squealed with delight.

"And sunk his teeth into your neck," added Marcy in a dramatic, goth kind of way.

We all shrieked with delight. But then I grew serious again. "Of course when I bumped into Jack and everybody I couldn't introduce Robert. And now it's a nightmare. I've ruined any chance I had with him." I flopped back down on my chair and stuffed fries into my mouth.

"No prob," said Luzie. "I'll tell Joey what the real deal is. And he'll tell Jack. Then everything will be fine again." She slapped her iPod headphones back onto her ears, and her gaze turned inward as the music filled her brain.

"Consider it handled," said Marcy.

"It'll be good for Jack to feel some jealousy, anyway. Keep him on his toes. He never knows when some fabulous movie star might just steal you away," said Kiki. She laughed and swung the beads of her chunky necklace in some kind of victory twirl.

I wanted to believe them, to believe that it would be so simple but I couldn't help feeling it would be way more complicated. I wasn't sure if I could ever look at Jack again.

"And while that all works itself out, we have a column to research," added Marcy. "'I Heart Robert Pattinson.' I can't wait. Did you know he sings as well as acts? I think he writes his own stuff too. I'll look into that side of him."

"And Luzie can research everything about *Harry Potter*. You know how she loves anything magical. Robert was amazing as Cedric Diggory. That scene makes me cry every time," babbled

Kiki. "Which leaves us with *Twilight*—yay! I'll watch the movie…again…and you can trawl the Internet for info on Rob. OK?"

"Forget the Internet. Harlee's going to conduct a real live celebrity interview, right? And we're coming with her. Where's he staying?" asked Marcy.

Luckily at that moment the bell for classes rang, and I gobbled down my lunch, and my mouth was way too full of food to answer.

History class was a blur. I watched Jack come in with Toby but as he walked towards his desk I ducked my head into my bag to search for non-existent homework. By the time my head was free and clear again he was sitting down, his back to me. I was getting to know his back quite well, the way his hair curled up on one side, and one of his ears leaned slightly away from the side of his head. *A perfect imperfection*. Then my mind went back to yesterday and Robert Pattinson's arm pressed around my shoulders, and my thoughts circled far away from the history of the French Revolution.

"Harlee Harte!" A deep voice cut harshly into my day dreams. I blinked. Mr. Thomas was yelling at me. Had I been texting without even knowing? I sat up straight. "Are you with us, Miss Harte, here in the land of the living? Or are you off in your very own Twilight zone?" The whole class was looking at me, laughing. *Even Jack with his lop-sided grin.* I felt myself blush. "Please do me the courtesy of opening your text book to page 347, and start reading the first paragraph out loud." I wanted to escape, to run to the girls' room, but instead I started to read, my face burning, Jack's laughter ringing in my ears.

At the lockers I waited for Kiki, Marcy, and Luzie so we could work out our plans. They didn't seem to be around, which was strange, but there was a huge crowd of girls blocking the way through. Younger kids, like 7th and 8th grade. Was there a bake sale or something? But then they started pointing at me and whispering, and one of them, Sarah, I think, came up to me. "Can you get Robert

Pattinson's autograph?" I stared at her, speechless. This was happening to me a lot lately. "You're going out with him, right?" I nearly choked. The crowd of girls was getting bigger, murmuring towards me, and they all seemed to be saying, "Edward, Edward, Edward." I was stuck in a crowd of crazy Twilighters! I wanted it to be a dream or a nightmare, but I wasn't waking up. "No, no," I managed to say. "Of course, I'm not." But no one seemed to be listening.

Finally I saw Marcy's head at the back of the crowd and waved at her. Thank goodness she is so tall. She shrugged and grimaced in an unhelpful kind of way, but then I saw her striding through the crowd. "Make way, make way," she yelled, and behind her were Kiki and Luzie, holding back the chanting, swaying girls until they reached me. Then they bundled me in between them, and we ran, and shoved and tripped our way out of school and around the corner onto Sunset Boulevard.

"My legs are weak," I said, starting to giggle uncontrollably.

"That was intense," agreed Marcy.

"Oh, no, here they come," hissed Kiki. "They're following us." We took off down the street, Luzie in the lead, and I swear I felt like we had gained vampire powers because I had never run so fast before. Even Kiki kept up. We reached my house and collapsed inside the front door, and fell on the floor laughing.

"This is not funny," I said.

"I know," said Kiki. "It's serious." But then she was laughing again.

"What happened to handling it?" I asked. "Why does the whole school think I'm dating a movie star? What is wrong with everyone?"

"Well, I told Joey the truth, and he got it and thought it was cool, and he told his friends. And, I guess somehow the story got changed and rumors started to spread, and now you're the It girl of Hollywoodland High."

"Maybe someone spread the rumors on purpose," said Marcy suddenly. "To make you look bad. Maybe."

"But who? And why?"

"I don't know. Someone else who has a crush on Jack. Or someone who has a crush on you, Harlee."

"Great," I said. "This would never have happened if I'd stayed home with Alec and played *Mutant Weasels from Mars*." This was complicated and scary, and the truth was getting lost somewhere in the middle. I started up the stairs to my bedroom. "And what about Jack?"

I didn't really want to know the answer. He probably hated me now.

"Joey told him the truth. It's up to him what he wants to believe. I mean it's not like you've been behaving differently towards him, right?"

"No," I said. But I knew that wasn't true. I'd been avoiding him all day. What was he supposed to think? "Well, I can't worry about this right now. I can work out Jack tomorrow. But I have to get this column researched." I pulled out my binder of notes from the night before, and my friends settled down at my computer.

"Look, here's his playlist," Marcy said, pointing to the screen. "He's a Van Morrison fan... that's so awesome."

"Who's Van Morrison? Luzie asked, but dropped the question when Marcy gave her a "you've got to be kidding" look.

"Whoa, did you know there was a petition against Robert Pattinson when he was cast as Edward Cullen?" asked Kiki, looking up from the screen.

"When are you going to interview him, Harlee?" Luzie ventured.

It was the one question I had dreaded. I didn't want to tell my friends that they couldn't come with me to meet him. But I had to.

"Yeah, I can drive us over there," said Kiki excitedly, always eager to drive now that she had her license.

"He asked me to keep the name of his hotel secret," I explained. "I can't tell you, and I can't bring you with me."

♡ Robert's Playlist ♡

VAN MORRISON: An Irish singer-songwriter whose career has spanned five decades. Robert says that he inspired him to play music in the first place. He has seen him at least six times in concert and owns every album. Van Morrison's brand of music has influenced many musicians. It is described as Celtic soul and encompasses jazz, soul, and rhythm and blues.

JEFF BUCKLEY: Robert's singing style has been compared to this guitarist-singer from California. Buckley spent his early years as a musician singing and playing guitar at a small Irish café in New York, playing folk, rock, and blues. He went on to get himself a record deal and toured Europe attracting attention and critical acclaim, but drowned at the age of thirty. Robert would love to play him in a movie.

KINGS OF LEON: a Grammy-winning alternative rock band.

JAMES BROWN: Known as "The Godfather of Soul" music, Brown has influenced many musicians with his singing, songwriting, and dancing.

CURTIS MAYFIELD: An American soul, R&B, and funk singer, songwriter, and record producer. He played many instruments too—the guitar, bass, piano, saxophone, and drums.

JOHNNY FLYNN: a musician friend of Robert who grew up in London with him. Johnny is with the English folk rock band called Johnny Flynn & The Sussex Wit. Johnny is also a poet and an actor and acts in a theater group.

"That's mean. He's an actor. He should deal with it," said Kiki. "If you can't handle the heat…"

"Stay out of the kitchen," continued Luzie. "What's the point of being famous if you're going to lock yourself up in a hotel? Kiki's right, he should deal with it."

"He does deal with it," I said. "He goes on talk shows and autograph signings and does press conferences. He does a lot for his fans. But maybe he just wants to have a private life sometimes and hang out with his BFFs and order in Chinese food."

"I'm with him," said Marcy. "You go alone. But we want autographs and photos. We'll be here when you get back—and speaking of Chinese, can you bring us some?"

I gave all my friends a hug. They were the best.

My mom just raised her eyebrows when I said I was on a top secret assignment and asked her if she could she drive me to the Sofitel, wait for me, then drive me back. I figure she'll be happy when I get my driver's license.

"It's for my column," I added. She nodded. "I wish you'd put as much time into your school work as you do your writing assignments for the newspaper."

As we pulled out of the driveway, she asked, "Who else is in on this secret assignment?"

"No one," I said. "Why?"

"Oh. But the car parked outside the house with those girls in it. They're not part of this?"

I twisted around in my seat trying to see what she was talking about. She was right. There was a car crammed with girls in it behind us. I recognized a couple of them from school.

"They're following us," said Mom.

"For real?" I gasped.

Mom checked her mirror again and nodded. She took a left onto La Cienega. "They're still with us. Maybe they're spies from another newspaper."

"Or maybe just a group of crazy *Twilight* fans." I sighed. "Do me a favor, Mom. Change of plan. Drop me at the Four Seasons for a few minutes instead. Thanks."

Later that night...

I was hanging out with my friends eating chicken with cashew nuts and watching *Twilight*. So what if I didn't get to interview Robert Pattinson. Life was still good. Until I started thinking about other things, and then it got confusing, and panic set in. How could I find out if Jack still liked me? Or had ever liked me? I groaned and took another mouthful of rice.

The next morning at the library...

Even before I could get out of my chair to go to the printer Toby ran up with my hot just-off-the-press column. "Oh, thanks," I said. "I didn't see you there."

"Well, you looked pretty intense while you were typing. Guess you were really into your subject."

"Very funny, Toby. You don't believe those rumors do you?"

"Relax, Harlee. No, I don't. I already checked your neck for vampire bites." He grinned and dodged just as I threw my sandal at him. "How do you wear these things?" he asked picking it up and disappearing through the library door with it. Before I could react...

"Harlee!" What now? I turned to see Philip Pendleton IV striding towards me, his tweed jacket open. "Thought I might find you here hammering out your column. It's finished, I take it? It would be a shame if Sondra had to take over as celebrity reporter."

"Yes, it's finished. And, don't worry, it's really good. Sondra will just have to spend all her spare time shopping as usual."

"One last thing, Harlee. You're not really dating the subject of this week's celebrity column, are you?" I rolled my eyes. Was he going to talk to me about professionalism and journalistic ethics?

"Of course not," I said.

"Oh, good," he said. Then he flushed, fumbled with his glasses, and walked off. I stared after him. Did he just sigh with relief? No, that would be too weird. Before I could get my head around the possibility that Philip Pendleton IV might possibly like me, I found myself looking into the blue eyes of Jack. He was smiling at me. I allowed myself to smile back. He must have heard my whole conversation with Philip. Life was good again. *Even with just one shoe.*

Later...

Mrs. Marshall walked to the podium in a yellow twin-set and jolted everyone awake with a squeal from the microphone.

"Good afternoon, students. As you know we have a fabulous event today, Professor Slitherwitch and her dancing pythons. But before you sit back and enjoy the show, I'd like to make an announcement. A letter arrived by messenger in my office this morning, and I'm going to read it to you as it concerns our very own Harlee Harte."

All eyes turned on me, and I wanted to slither away like one of the upcoming pythons, but then Mrs. Marshall was rattling on again.

"It is a letter from a Robert Pattinson. He says…" At this point her voice was drowned out by shrieks and squeals, and one of the younger girls appeared to faint and was carried out. Finally, everyone settled down, and she continued:

'"Thank you to Harlee Harte for being just complicated enough to be interesting but not too much to be weird. You are the best celebrity reporter in town. I know you didn't spill my secret address because I've been safe here from paparazzi and squealing fans. Thank you. Integrity is cool, and you're a cool girl. I hope that boy you like knows it. Maybe I'll write a song about you one day. Say hi to Alec for me. RP"'

Next to me Kiki, Marcy, and Luzie were clapping and yelling, and the whole school seemed to be cheering. Maybe it was nice to have fans once in a while. Especially if one of them turned out to be Jack Kelly.

PART TWO
The Column

THE HOLLYWOODLAND ST★R

VOL. 11 ISSUE 5

HOLLYWOOD, CA

Robert's BD:
May 13, 1986

Robert's Sign:
TAURUS
April 21 – May 21

Element: Earth

Ruling Planet:
Venus

Symbol:
The Bull

Stone:
Emerald

Life Pursuit:
Emotional and
Financial
Security

Vibration:
Determined
Energy

Secret Desire:
To have secure
happy life

HARTEBEAT

by Harlee Harte

I ♡ Robert Pattinson.

I guess we all think we know Robert Pattinson as the beautiful and mysterious Edward Cullen, vampire of our dreams and star of the movie *Twilight*, but as I was lucky enough to find out a couple of days ago, there is a really great guy behind Edward. A guy with a heartbeat! This week's column is dedicated to Robert Pattinson who handles his newfound fame pretty well.

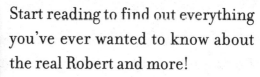

Start reading to find out everything you've ever wanted to know about the real Robert and more!

Young Robert

Robert Thomas Pattinson was born in England on May 13, 1986, and spent his entire childhood in Barnes, a leafy suburb, just southwest of London. His father, Richard, imported vintage cars from the United States, and his mother, Clare, worked with a modeling agency. He is the youngest of three children. His sister, Victoria, is five years older while Lizzy is three years older. Apparently his older siblings loved to dress him up as a girl and introduce him as their younger

Traits:
Rebellious

Like creature comforts

Social but like to withdraw into themselves

Determined

Have deep feelings and fears, often hidden

Female Celeb Taurus:
Lily Allen
Nikki Reed
Kelly Clarkson
Megan Fox

45

sister, Claudia. But that was a long time ago! Victoria now works in advertising, and Lizzy has found her own brand of fame as a singer with the band Aurora UK. She was spotted by a talent scout for a record company while singing at the local pub. As you'll discover, musical talent—and success— runs in the Pattinson family.

At the age of six Robert started at the Tower House, a private school for boys just a short drive away from home. As the school secretary, Caroline Booth, told the *London Evening Standard*, he was "an absolutely lovely boy, everyone adored him. We have lots of lovely boys here but he was something special. He was very pretty, beautiful and blond." Obviously his movie-star potential was apparent at a very young age! At Tower House Robert acted in several productions, his first role being the King of Hearts (awww!) in a play, *Spell for a Rhyme*, penned by a teacher of the school. Next he played Robert in an adaptation of William Golding's *Lord of the Flies*. Caroline Booth continued, "He wasn't a particularly academic child but he always loved drama." And a 1998 newsletter from Tower House described young Robert as "a runaway winner of last term's Form Three untidy desk award." It's good to know that even Robert isn't perfect.

At the age of twelve, Robert changed schools and started at The Harrodian School in Barnes. He has said that he was expelled from Tower House for being "quite bad" but it is unclear whether or not he was joking—and he likes to joke a lot. But it is sure that changing schools was a turning point for him as he has told *CBBC*, "I moved to a mixed school and then I became cool and discovered hair gel." Which he's been using ever since, it seems. At school, he doesn't seem to have been very interested in academics. His school reports were never very impressive—they usually said he didn't try very hard—and he rarely did his homework. He always turned up for school, however, as he liked his teachers. Recently he told the *London Evening Standard*, "I wasn't at all focused at school, and I didn't achieve much." But he seems to be sorry that he didn't achieve his potential there as he continued, "I've got a sense of urgency now. I feel I can't let any more time waste away."

Robert started his short modeling career at about this time through his mother's connections with the modeling agency where she worked, and he did several photo shoots for designers and clothing lines as well as spreads in teen magazines. He has said that he was really skinny and looked like a girl which was the in look at the time, but as he grew older—and became more manly—the work dried up. In modeling anyway.

Check it out!

Robert's nicknames are Rob, Patty, RPattz and Spunk Ransome. This last one came about during an MTV interview in which Robert said he didn't like his name and wished fans would invent a new one like…Spunk Ransome.

But Robert didn't mind as he had other interests to occupy his time. Outside of school he had joined a local theater group, the Barnes Theatre Group, at the insistence of his dad, and in the hope of meeting pretty girls. The club put on high-quality plays and was run by actors, so it was a great place to learn about all aspects of the theater. In the beginning Rob decided he would work backstage and help out with sets and the technical side of things. And there his talents may have festered if he hadn't decided to try out for a production of *Guys and Dolls* and landed a part in the chorus, "an embarrassing Cuban dancer part," but a part nonetheless. From there he went on to secure the lead role of George Gibbs in his next play, American playwright Thornton Wilder's *Our Town*. This may have been the first time that he used an American accent onstage. By now Robert had caught the acting bug, and he performed in many productions at the Barnes Theatre Club and also at The Old Sorting Office, another local theater. His productions included the musical *Anything Goes*, Shakespeare's *Macbeth*, in which he played the noble Malcolm, King of Scotland, and *Tess of the D'Urbervilles*. This production was especially important in his acting career as he played the charming but dangerous Alec Stoke d'Urberville and, after one of his performances, he was approached by a talent agent. This would then set him on the road to bigger things.

Even now that he is a worldwide phenomenon and mobbed by screaming fans wherever he goes, Robert remembers where he comes from and says, "I wouldn't be acting if it wasn't for the Barnes Theatre Club.... I owe everything to that little club." It is part of Robert's charm to be honest and unpretentious.

Check it out!

Sometimes Robert Pattinson thinks about giving up acting but then he realizes "I could be working in a shoe shop, acting is much cooler."

Pattinson has said that his favorite actor, and his early acting inspiration, is Jack Nicholson. He told *The London Evening Standard*, "I aspire to be Jack Nicholson. I love his every single mannerism." When he was about thirteen, just a couple of years before starting out at the Barnes Theatre Group, he watched the 1975 classic movie, *One Flew Over the Cuckoo's Nest*, starring Nicholson as Randle Patrick McMurphy, a patient who rebels against the rules of a mental asylum. From this point on, Pattinson became a huge Nicholson fan and has said that he used to dress like him, experiment with his accent, do everything like him. Over the years he has watched every single one of his movies. Within a few short years he would take these aspirations from the Barnes Theatre Group into the bigger world beyond.

Now that he had an agent Robert could branch out from local theater and look for professional roles in the world of television and movies. It wasn't long before he landed his first TV role in a German production called *Ring of the Nibelungs* (known here as *Dark Kingdom: The Dragon King*), based on the Germanic and Nordic myths that had inspired J.R.R. Tolkien to write *The Hobbit* and *The Lord of the Rings*. Robert played the part of Prince Giselher in this fantasy and spent over three months filming in South Africa.

At age seventeen, he lived there alone and learned not only what it was like to work on a movie set but also the value of independence. He also earned some money. And it's very interesting that his father made him pay his own school fees with his earnings. As Robert was still not especially academic at school and never really seemed to work hard, his dad suggested that he leave school and do something else as he wasn't willing to pay school fees any longer (in England you can finish school at 16, or you can stay on for two more years to take exams to continue on to university). But Robert wanted to take his exams so he agreed to pay his own fees. His parents have always kept Robert and his sisters down-to-earth, instilling a good work ethic in them and encouraging them to pay their way through part-time jobs. Robert had a paper route at the age of ten and made about 10 pounds ($17) a week.

Robert's *Harry Potter* days

Another important event happened around the time of the *Ring of the Nibelungs*. The day before he flew to South Africa, Robert had a meeting, arranged by his agent, with Mike Newell, director of *Harry Potter and the Goblet of Fire*. Robert was so excited to be heading off to South Africa that he had a great, confident meeting with the director, and when he returned to London, over three months later, he was invited to a call-back audition. There Mike Newell informed Robert that he had won the part of Cedric Diggory in the upcoming Potter flick. Later Newell told the *Evening Standard*, "Cedric exemplifies all that you would expect the Hogwarts champion to be. Robert Pattinson was born to play the role; he's quintessentially English with chiseled public schoolboy good looks."

But first, before he could embark on *Goblet of Fire* Robert had another job in the movie *Vanity Fair* as actress Reese Witherspoon's son. Unfortunately, Rob's scenes didn't make it to the final cut of the movie but ended up on the cutting room floor. Rob has always wondered if he was too old to play Reese's son as she was only twenty-seven at the time of filming. Fortunately, if you really want to see him in this movie you can find him in the DVD version.

Then he also had a little something called EXAMS that he had to get through. Somehow, despite his reputation for not working hard at school, he managed to do well in them, and then he could put school behind him and concentrate on the parts of his life that he really loved—and excelled at.

Robert's role as Cedric Diggory was the part of a lifetime for a young and fairly inexperienced actor, and it would challenge Robert in many ways. First, he would be filming for almost a year with an already established team of some of England's most prestigious actors and actresses—Maggie Smith (Professor McGonagall), Michael Gambon (Dumbledore), Gary Oldman (Sirius Black), Ralph Fiennes (Voldemort), Miranda Richardson (Rita Skeeter)—as well as the iconic young actors who had taken England by storm playing Harry, Hermione, and Ron (Daniel Radcliffe, Emma Watson, and Rupert Grint). Second, there were huge box-office expectations placed upon the shoulders of this movie with its $75 million budget. And, third, there were the fans—fans of J.K. Rowling's incredibly popular Harry Potter novels as well as fans of the previous movies. These fans knew every single detail of the books and wrote about them on their own Web sites and fanzines, and they had very strong opinions on how a character should and should not be played. This would not be Robert's only experience with fans as we shall see. And this was all before the movie even opened in theaters. After that, there would be other challenges for Robert to face. He did not know it in March 2004 when filming on the movie began, but life was never going to be quite the same for him again.

As all Harry Potter-philes know, Cedric Diggory is the crush-worthy star of the Huffle-Puff Quidditch team and a Head Boy as well. He's an all-around good guy: hard-working and honest and, of course, hot. He's a natural, then, to represent Hogwarts in the Tri-Wizard Tournament, and when his name bursts from the goblet of fire as the chosen one, he has the backing of the whole school community. Then when poor Harry's name is conjured up too, an unpleasant rivalry starts up— against the better nature of the two boys. So what did Robert Pattinson think of Cedric Diggory? He told *CBBC* (children's *BBC*), "I think Cedric's a

pretty cool character. He's not really a complete cliché of the good kid in school. He's just quiet. He is actually just a genuinely good person, but he doesn't make a big deal about it or anything. He's just like, 'Whatever.' I can kind of relate to that."
And how similar was Robert Pattinson to Cedric Diggory? Well, knowing what we do about Robert's school days they probably weren't very alike. When he was a lunch monitor he stole people's French fries. He told the *Evening Standard*, "I was never a leader, and the idea of my ever being made head boy would have been a complete joke. I wasn't involved in much at school, and I was never picked for any of the teams." (Until Team Edward came along later…)

And what about the fact that in the book and the script Cedric is described as "an absurdly handsome seventeen-year-old?" As we know, it wouldn't be the last time that Robert would have to play someone so beautiful. Robert is very modest and humble about most of his talents and especially about his good looks, so it's not surprising that he told *CBBC*: "It kind of puts you off a little bit when you're trying to act, and you're trying to get good angles to look good-looking and stuff…. It's much scarier than meeting Voldemort." And yet he does it so well.

Before the shooting of the movie started, director Mike Newell had the idea of getting the young actors and actresses to spend two weeks together so they could all get to know each other, and so that the newcomers would feel at home and not under too much pressure from the already established actors. It turned out to be an awesome plan. They spent the weeks on physical exercises and improvisation exercises, had a lot of fun, and somewhere during those two weeks everyone became a team. Robert especially enjoyed hanging out with Rupert Grint who plays red-headed cutie Ron Weasley in the movies. He is apparently as funny in real life as on-screen. Robert also became friends with newcomers Stanislav Ianevski

(Durmstrang champion, Viktor Krum) and Katie Leung (who plays Cedric's girlfriend, Cho Chang). As Tri-Wizard champions, he and Stan were often in scenes together while he and Katie had to dance together and hold hands a lot, but most of his big scenes involved Daniel Radcliffe. In the beginning Robert admits to having been intimidated by Radcliffe, not because he wasn't friendly, but because he was Harry Potter!

Robert also admits that at first, while he was still getting used to being part of such a big production—some days there would be over 2000 people on set—he wasn't really himself. Robert desired to be taken seriously as an actor so he used to sit around drinking coffee and trying to look really intense! Luckily he changed and began to feel more at home on the set. He also started to become more polite after playing Cedric Diggory, because that's just the way Cedric was.

One of the most exciting scenes in the movie is when Harry and Cedric are racing around inside the maze, trying to work out the riddles to win the tournament, and just get out of there alive. This scene was the first one that was filmed, and it took Dan and Robert two weeks of intense work. The maze was made with hydraulic walls that could be moved backwards and forwards, and filming took place by steadicam, in which someone just ran around filming with a camera. This was one of the most expensive parts of the movie—because of the maze—and one of the hardest to film. Rob also ended up with some cuts and bruises—and learned the importance of being able to turn to stunt doubles for help.

The whole movie is filled with pretty intense action, and the work was physically demanding for all the actors, but especially for the tournament champions. Cedric, as a Quidditch star, was expected to look very healthy, and so Robert was started on a physical exercise program with a personal trainer, one of the stunt doubles. He found the work incredibly difficult as he had not been keeping fit before, but he did manage to get in shape enough—until he hurt his shoulder exercising, and it was decided that Cedric would have to be fine just the way he was.

For the second of the magical tasks in the movie, Robert—and the other young actors—worked on swimming and diving, and he learned how to scuba-dive. He admits that he could barely swim before preparing for the underwater scenes—although he said in his audition that he could. In these scenes, some of the most intense in the movie, the champions each have to rescue a loved one from the bottom of the Black Lake on the Hogwarts' school grounds, a lake filled with aggressive mermaids and other magical creatures. To do so they have to dive into icy water and make their way through murky darkness and underwater vegetation, past unknown creatures. Cedric's task is to find his girlfriend Cho. The actors spent two months filming these sequences. They practiced their underwater swimming in a small tank, but the actual scenes were shot in an enormous specially-constructed, 36-foot, deep tank which was very different and hard to get used to at first. Not only was it difficult for the actors to swim and act at the same time, but they had to do so without breathing. They were given breaths of oxygen by divers in the tank with them. While finding the underwater acting challenging at first, Robert grew to like it, finding it easy to focus on the work as there were no distractions, and eventually even describing it as "calming." (*CBBC*)

Harry Potter and the Goblet of Fire was the first in the series of Harry Potter books (and movies) in which a main character dies, and so there was a lot of talk before the movie's release about how this scene would be handled, and how young audiences would react. In 2008, *Entertainment Weekly* ranked the death scene as number four in their "Twenty Five New Classic Death Scenes" list. As it is Cedric Diggory who dies, meeting his untimely death at the hands of Voldemort and Peter Pettigrew in an emotional graveyard scene, Robert Pattinson found himself and his character at the center of much attention. At first, Pattinson was upset that his character was going to be killed off. He told *The London Evening Standard*, "I looked at the other actors, and thought, 'God! Lucky you! You've got another three films guaranteed!'" But once he had come to terms with Cedric's death, he looked forward to the filming of this scene. Many actors have to wait years before getting a good death scene to play!

In both the book and the movie, this scene is incredibly emotional as Harry and Cedric decide to share the glory of winning the tournament after fighting against each other in the maze. They grasp the champion's cup together, expecting to raise it in victory, but instead are transported to a dismal graveyard where Voldemort and his loyal followers await them. With a jolt, reader and audience realize that Cedric is very out-of-place in this world, and within moments he is dead, not needed by

Voldemort and felled by Peter Pettigrew's "Avada Kadavra" killing spell. Robert Pattinson's portrayal of Cedric made him into more than a jock, more than a good guy: he seemed to stand for youthful vitality in direct contrast to Voldemort's ugly evil vision of the world. He lies dead as Harry desperately battles Voldemort, as Harry's parents emerge from Voldemort's wand, and finally as Harry lunges, risking all, to bring Cedric's body home to Hogwarts. It is an emotional scene. And Robert Pattinson is at its center.

While the cemetery scene was one that Robert enjoyed, the one that he found most difficult, or at least most embarrassing, was the Yule Ball. Apparently, the ballroom dancing aspect was fine as everybody knew exactly what they were supposed to be doing, and Robert was able to waltz with his partner. But when the crew told everyone to "just dance" to the rock band it was "really awkward." (*CBBC*)

Of all the distinguished actors that Pattinson acted with on the set of *Goblet of Fire*, the one who intimidated him most was Ralph Fiennes who played Lord Voldemort. One of his favorite actors was Warwick Davis (Professor Flitwick) whom he had watched over and over when younger as Willow Ufgood in the movie *Willow*. But it was typical of Robert that when sitting next to the actor he was too shy to think of anything to say to him.

In November 2005 the movie was released, and Robert's world changed. At the movie's London premiere he described that the day before he had been sitting in London's Leicester Square "happily being ignored by everyone. Then suddenly strangers are screaming your name." He walked up the red carpet with the other stars for the world premiere in front of thousands of screaming fans and a throng of paparazzi and suddenly realized what it meant to be part of the Harry Potter franchise, part of something huge. It seemed that from that moment on everyone knew his name.

The movie was wildly successful among fans and critics alike and grossed over \$896 million worldwide. *The London Evening Standard* said, "He is one of the bright new stars of the latest Harry Potter film. Now Robert Pattinson is being dubbed 'the next Jude Law' for a screen-stealing performance as the dashing head boy in *Harry Potter And The Goblet Of Fire*. The London-born teenager, who plays Potter's love rival, will set hearts racing among female cinema-goers when the film is released tomorrow."

Consequently, he was named as 2005's *British Star of Tomorrow* by London Times Online, stating "This fresh-faced, photogenic eighteen-year old so oozes charm and likeability that casting directors are predicting a big future." They were right! Robert Pattinson's career was launched. He had proven that he could take a small but important role in an epic movie and pull it off. Now he was ready for anything.

Twilight time

Pattinson didn't rush into another big-budget movie immediately. He did sign up with a US-based agent, and he did go to meetings and auditions in LA, but nothing seemed right for him, and so he didn't sign on for anything. Instead he went back to London and lived with a friend in a rented apartment and recovered from the exhaustion of the Potter shoot and its aftermath. He told the *Philadelphia Daily News*, "I didn't do anything for a year, I just sat on the roof and played music." This laid-back attitude would turn out to be typical Pattinson too. Well, he did decide to do a play in London's West End, a German play titled *The Woman Before*, but somehow he got himself fired before the play opened, or he pulled out of the production. It is not quite clear which but, either way, he never graced the stage.

Check it out!

When Robert Pattinson was younger his dream job was to be a pianist in a piano bar.

Robert only took on one role in the whole of 2006, the year after *Goblet of Fire*, and this was a television movie for the *BBC*, *The Haunted Airman*. He played the role of Toby Jugg, a World War Two pilot who is shot and paralyzed, and eventually goes mad. It was a depressing role, but one that Pattinson played with great sensitivity. A review in *The Stage* wrote "Pattinson —an actor whose jaw line is so finely chiseled it could split granite—played the airman...with a perfect combination of youthful terror and world-weary cynicism."

Next Robert took on another obscure part in another British television movie, *The Bad Mother's Handbook*, in which he was cast as a shy young man who befriends a pregnant girl. Not exactly an epic movie, but this would be another example of Robert working on projects he found meaningful rather than obvious moneymakers. He was not always one to seek out the Hollywood spotlight.

His next projects, *The Summer House*, *How to Be* and *Little Ashes* were equally low-budget movies, taken on by Robert because he thought they seemed interesting and wouldn't typecast him as a Cedric Diggory. And I will tell you about these projects. But later. Because before these movies could be released something happened to Robert Pattinson, something even bigger than Harry Potter, that catapulted him into the forefront of megastardom. He became Edward Cullen, hottest vampire ever, which, of course, is why he has to sneak around town these days, hoodie pulled up to hide his unmistakable hair, dreamy eyes, and killer grin.... But, sorry, I digress.

Let's backtrack a few years to 2005 when Stephenie Meyer's vampire novel, *Twilight*, was published. Almost overnight the novel captured the hearts and souls of millions of teenage girls—and women—(and a few men) worldwide. They loved the romance of the book, the *Romeo and Juliet* intensity of the love affair. And these fans had one thing in common. They adored Edward Cullen, the enigmatic, handsome vampire who falls in love with Bella Swan, a mere mortal. And they especially liked the fact that his love is doomed because at the center of his feeling of intense passion for Bella is his equally intense desire to kill her. Yet Bella loves him too. The chemistry between them is magnetic, and there is nothing that can stop them from feeling the way they do about each other.

It is easy to find Edward attractive with his money and sports car and flawless looks, his cat-like speed, his strength that enables him to stop a car with his bare hands. But it is his unconditional love for Bella, his desire to protect her, his kindness, and his manners that had so many clamoring to join Team Edward. And fans joined the team in their millions. They created Web sites and fan pages and connected in a formidable mass with ideas and opinions about the world of *Twilight* and their need to obsess over everything Edward. The Twilighters or Twihards were born. Author, Stephenie Meyer, wrote to her fans and commented on their Web sites, turned up at their gatherings and proms until she and her fans and the world that she had created were interconnected in a way that had never happened before. *Twilight* had turned into a phenomenon.

In July 2007 Stephenie Meyer and Summit Entertainment announced that *Twilight* (the book) would become *Twilight* (the movie) as it would be going into production with Catherine Hardwicke as director. Catherine had directed, among other films, *Lords of Dogtown*, *The Nativity Story*, and *Thirteen*, and she loved the book. At Comic Con she said, "I fell in love with Stephenie's world the first time I read it, it's like I'm there! I want to see it, I want to breathe it in and see it come to life." As director, one of the first things Catherine did was to oversee the writing of the screenplay—the transformation of the novel into a script that would depict the world of *Twilight* on the big screen. She wanted Forks, Washington, from the novel to be instantly recognizable in her movie version. Her other main focus was the transformation of the characters from novel to bigscreen. As the action in *Twilight* unfolds through Bella's eyes, Catherine decided it made sense to work first on casting an actress to play the role of Bella Swan. Her first choice was Kristen Stewart, whom she had recently seen and admired in the movie *Into the Wild*, in which she plays a young woman in love with a guy who has left society behind in search of a more real existence. Catherine flew to Pittsburgh where Kristen was filming *Adventureland* and did an impromptu screen test of her jumping on a bed and chasing pigeons. Even before she made it back home to LA, she knew she had found her Bella, and with Bella in place she could turn her attention to casting Edward.

This turned out to be a much more complicated, drawn-out affair. And this is where Robert comes in. Not only, did it seem, did everyone want to play the part of Edward, but everyone had their own idea of Edward. Girls and women all over the world had their own ideal Edwards. Stephenie Meyer has always said that she wanted the actor Henry Cavill (*The Tudors*) to play the part, but by the time auditions took place he was already 24 years old and too old to play the eternally 17-year-old Mr. Cullen. So she and Catherine had to focus their attention elsewhere, poring over books of headshots, looking at over 3000 resumes that were sent in by agents and casting directors, trying to find the perfect Edward.

In England, Robert Pattinson had been sent the *Twilight* script by his agent, and he liked the fact that it was action-filled, but he was very nervous about Edward's physical perfection. He wasn't sure how he would play Edward and was embarrassed by the idea of showing up at an audition to try out for the role of "Mr. Perfect." There's that shy guy again. In his interview with the *Sunday Paper* he said, "Edward's described as this perfect man, with an impeccable face and body. Everything about him is just amazing. There's no way I could ever live up to that." However, luckily, his agent persuaded him to overcome his modesty and fly out to LA to meet with Catherine Hardwicke and Kristin Stewart and to just give it a go. After all, what was there to lose?

He turned up for the audition at Catherine's house in Venice, California, and was asked to read a couple of scenes. Then, with Kristen, he was asked to act out a love scene—on Catherine's bed—in which Edward has to control the dangerous passion he feels for Bella, a passion if truly unleashed could result in Bella's death. Catherine's idea was to see the compatibility between Robert and Kristen as, obviously, Edward and Bella's love story is the essence of the entire movie. And she loved what she saw (and the rest is history!) Robert has said that he was inspired by the way in which

Kristen played Bella—as strong and intelligent, not at all the insipid female character he was expecting—and it brought out a different Edward in him—a tortured Edward with a broken soul. This was what Catherine—and Kristen—loved. According to Catherine in *GQ*, Robert brought a different layer to Edward's personality. She said, "I'd seen a zillion really cute guys. But that was the problem. They all looked like the super-cute kid in your high school. The prom king, or the captain of the football team. They didn't look like they were from another world and time." Kristen agreed saying, "Everybody came in doing something empty and shallow and thoughtless—but Rob understood that it wasn't a frivolous role." When she said to Catherine, "It has to be Rob," the search for Edward was over, and Robert Pattinson was signed up.

Stephenie Meyer's statement on her Web site was extremely enthusiastic: "I am ecstatic with Summit's choice for Edward. There are very few actors who can look both dangerous and beautiful at the same time, and even fewer who I can picture in my head as Edward. Robert Pattinson is going to be amazing." Yet, almost immediately, there was trouble in store for the young actor. Stephenie's fans did not approve of the choice of Robert Pattinson as their beloved Edward Cullen, and blogs and Web sites twittered with outrage. Over 75,000 fans signed a petition asking for anyone other than Robert Pattinson as Edward, and Robert's mom e-mailed him links to Web sites where his looks and acting ability were completely trashed. Thanks Mom! But Robert managed to take it all in his stride. Obviously he would have loved to have been embraced from the very beginning but he realized—sensibly—that you can't please everyone, and his attitude was to prove all the nay-sayers wrong. And he would.

Robert prepared intensely for his role as Edward by heading out to Portland, Oregon, alone, two months ahead of the rest of the cast and crew.

Oregon was chosen because of its often overcast weather which would be perfect for bringing to life the world of *Twilight* in which vampires can never go out in the sunlight. There, he distanced himself from friends and family in an effort to understand Edward's character better and to feel his desperate isolation. For that is how Robert had always viewed Edward: an immortal tragic figure who doesn't have much to live for and yet cannot escape the world. His feelings towards Bella are intensely complicated: murderous desire combined with romantic love. An impossible love. "He's a guy," said Robert of Edward, "who's just incredibly frustrated and he finds this one thing which is his and he can't keep it safe, and that's almost impossible for him to handle."

Just as he had to for *Goblet of Fire*, Robert needed to reach a high level of physical fitness for his role as Edward, and he worked out intensively at a local gym for a couple of months. In fact, he worked so hard that he was told to stop, and

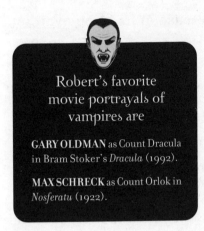

Robert's favorite movie portrayals of vampires are

GARY OLDMAN as Count Dracula in Bram Stoker's *Dracula* (1992).

MAX SCHRECK as Count Orlok in *Nosferatu* (1922).

to go out and eat cheeseburgers which Robert loved because he is a big fan of fast-food. Seeing as he was playing the impossibly handsome Edward, Robert had to be just perfect, and so it was suggested, before shooting began, that he have some work done on his teeth. He complied and even wore braces to raise his already high level of perfection! One other physical transformation was necessary before Robert could step into Edward's shoes, and that was: contact lenses. Robert had to wear them every day of filming to change his own blue eyes into Edward's golden orbs. And even though he put the lenses in every morning, he never got used to it, and laughs that it would take him twenty minutes every morning. And, finally, there was his accent. Robert had to drop his sexy

British accent to take on Edward's all-American one. But Robert didn't need any voice training. He was able to channel all the American movies (especially those Jack Nicholson flicks) he grew up watching and come up with just the right accent for Edward. Although he has admitted that at first he would just use different actors' accents, and so his accent would change all the time, and that during exciting action sequences he would sound like Al Pacino!

Check it out!

Robert was supposed to have long, vampire hair for the movie, *Twilight*, and underwent eight hours of hairstyling to have extensions fitted. But he hated them, and so they were removed, and he was allowed to keep his own look.

In the end, Robert found it best to just use an American accent all the time, between takes and off the set, so that he didn't have to move in and out between American and English. He told MTV.com, "For the big dialogue scenes, it's just easier to not keep switching between. I kind of do it by accident. I keep forgetting that I'm speaking in an American accent sometimes. The dangerous thing is that you end up forgetting what your real accent is after awhile! It's really strange—I've never done a job in an American accent before."

While working out just how he was going to play Edward, Stephenie leant Robert several chapters of her unpublished novel, *Midnight Sun*. The novel is now available on the Internet after it was leaked—much to Stephenie's dismay—but during the filming of the movie it had only been shown to a handful of people. The novel tells the story of *Twilight* from Edward's point of view, instead of Bella's, and so it gives a powerful insight into Edward's mind and his tortured feelings on first setting his eyes on Bella. Robert has said that it made him understand how dangerous Edward really is, that he really does think about killing

Bella—and not just her, the whole school. It gave him a whole new perspective and deepened the layers of Edward's character so he could understand the monster beneath the charm. It is no surprise then that his favorite scene in the finished movie is not one of the fast-paced chase scenes or even the popular baseball scene but a relatively small sequence when Bella states, "I'm not scared of you. You're not a monster." It especially pleased Robert when he learned that this is one of Stephenie's favorite scenes too—proving that he had captured the Edward that she had set out to create years earlier.

One of the other elements of Edward's character that Robert had a hard time in understanding was his age. At first he couldn't work out why Edward, at the real age of over 100, would act as a seventeen-year-old, or pretend to be a seventeen-year-old to Bella—who knew he wasn't. He also thought that the Edward-Carlisle relationship is an interesting dynamic—why does Edward accept Carlisle as his father just because he saved him from the Spanish flu and transformed him into a vampire? Robert's constant questioning, and reading and re-reading of the scripts, *Twilight* and *Midnight Sun,* helped him to come to a deeper understanding of Edward's character that would show through in the movie.

There were plenty of action scenes to sink his teeth into, but Robert learned to allow stunt doubles to take on some of this work. However, he still needed to do some wire work, especially when sprinting at top vampire-speed. As many Twilighters will tell you, the scene in the book in which the Cullens play baseball in a thunderstorm (to hide the sounds of them hitting the ball) is a favorite. It allows a moment of light relief, when Bella is accepted into the Cullen family, before the horror of the arrival of James, the tracker vampire. After this scene the novel turns pretty scary. Likewise, in the movie, the baseball scene is extremely important—everything about it must work. And so, it was vital that Robert, who had grown up in England and had never played baseball in his life, could transform into the athletic and graceful Edward, god of the baseball diamond. Robert found the whole thing amusing. He told ReelzChannel, "I'm terrible. I'm completely mal-coordinated. I'm terrible at all sports.... I even had a baseball coach. Catherine was so determined to make me look like a professional baseball player..." Luckily, Robert seemed to learn everything he needed to know as he looks just fine rounding the bases on the big screen.

While Robert may not be much of an athlete, in his words at least, his musical talent was definitely present in the movie, proving that Robert is very much more than just a pretty face. Edward is an accomplished pianist, and Robert definitely did not need a double for this part of Edward's character. Two songs that he wrote and performed appear on *Twilight*'s soundtrack: "Never Think" and "Let Me Sign." Director Catherine had been told about Robert's musical abilities by

Kristen Stewart and Nikki Reed (who plays Rosalie Cullen) and constantly asked him to let her listen to something he'd written, but he was reluctant. Finally she convinced him to go into a friend's studio where he sang and played guitar, about six songs. Next she put them in a cut, and before Pattinson knew what was happening they were in the movie! The song, "Never Think," fits nicely with the restaurant scene where Edward and Bella have dinner together (well, she eats and he watches.) The lyrics, sung in a heartfelt whisper by Pattinson, are meaningful: "Girl save your soul, Before it's too far gone and before nothing can be done. Without me you got it all so hold on." "Let Me Sign" adds to the emotional intensity of Bella's death scene at the Ballet Studio. Even Robert agreed, although (with typical modesty) he tried not to have his name appear on the credits, but he didn't get his way there either. Catherine said in *Catherine Hardwicke's Twilight: Director's Notebook*, "One of my favorite days was watching Rob record.

He sang the songs dozens of times, but no two takes were alike. The music seemed to flow from somewhere deep inside." The sound track eventually went on to become Atlantic Records' best-selling sound track of all time. Robert has said that he would like to make his own album at some point, but probably independently and under a pseudonym. He doesn't want to cash in on the success of *Twilight* or use the movie as a way to jump-start his music career. Music will always be there for him. He told the *LA Times*, "Music is my backup plan if acting fails. I don't want to put all my eggs in one basket."

Robert started playing the piano at three or four (back at Tower House school) and the guitar at around age five. His music has been a constant in his life, something that he finds relaxing and inspiring, that he just can't be without. Remember that year he spent playing guitar on a London rooftop after the release of *Goblet of Fire*? He has played with a band in London and used to enjoy open mike sessions in various bars and pubs—until he became too famous and people started recording him and posting his sessions on YouTube. He describes his music as Van Morrison-ish, Jeff Buckley-ish and says he doesn't know much about contemporary music. He told ShowbizNest, "I do have an iPod but listen to a lot of old blues."

The *Twilight* soundtrack sold incredibly well and jump-started the careers of three musicians who were previously not very well known: Sam Bradley, Marcus Foster, and Bobby Long. All three of them are friends and musical collaborators with Robert Pattinson—Sam and Marcus went to school with him, and Bobby met up with him on the London music scene.

The song "Never Think" was co-written by Robert and Sam, and the song "Let Me Sign" was co-written by Marcus and Bobby. Now Sam, Marcus, and Bobby can count *Twilight* fans among their fans, and even have girls screaming at their concerts.

If you haven't checked out their music yet, you should —it's really good. All three musicians have MySpace sites where you can listen.

The *Twilight* phenomenon

Twilight was released in the US on November 21, 2008, and on its opening day earned almost $35.7 million. To date it has earned over $380,000,000 worldwide, not bad for a movie with a $37 million production budget. Overall, movie reviews were mixed, but in the end that didn't matter. The fans loved the movie, and almost overnight, Robert Pattinson became a megastar. This was different from his success with *Goblet of Fire*. There he was part of a moviemaking phenomenon, a franchise, and he was just one small part of it. With *Twilight* he had played a lead role: he had brought to life Edward Cullen and had gained himself millions of fans. Screaming, adoring fans. He had overcome their initial reserve, and now they followed him wherever he went on the movie's global press tour. Any privacy he had had was now a thing of the past.

Robert found himself on major TV talk shows (where it became clear he laughed a lot, had a great sense of humor, and didn't always give straight answers), his face was constantly splashed on the cover of magazines, and there were columns and columns of articles about him—with headings like "The Vampire Heartthrob," "Vampire Hunks," "50 Hollywood Hotties," and the no-pressure title "Drop Dead Dazzling." In reviews he was described as "the modern expression of vampirism. He's super strong yet delicate and…he is undeniably sexy." (*Hollywood Reporter*)

Entertainment Weekly described Edward as "Romeo, Heathcliff, James Dean, and Brad Pitt all rolled into one." Even Robert's hair became a major topic of conversation, especially that bashful way he had of running his hands through it. *Entertainment Weekly*'s November issue summed up the hype: "The Stars of Twilight. If the vampire movie explodes, so will their lives. Are they ready for fame?"

How did Robert handle all this sudden exposure? When he signed on for his role of Edward he had no idea of what he was getting into in terms of fan adoration. He had thought the movie—based on its budget and no big stars—was a low-key production. So when he found himself at the center of so much attention and adulation he was shocked—and a little scared. Stephenie Meyer told EW.com, "I asked the producer, 'Is Rob ready for this? Have you guys prepped him? Is he ready to be the It Guy?' I don't think he really is. I don't think he sees himself that way. And I think the transition is going to be a little rocky.'" She was right. In an interview with *Film Monthly* he said, "I don't know why it still shocks me. I mean, I've been going for the last three weeks, just going to different cities all around the world, just to get to these planned mobbing, where everybody just screams and screams and screams. But every single time, I get so nervous, and kind of cold sweats, and everything." From San Diego's Comic Con to New

York's Apple Store he is met by screaming fans that drown out questions and answers and don't seem to mind as long as they get to see a glimpse of him.

But, luckily, all the attention has not scared Robert away from signing up to play Edward in the *Twilight* sequels based on Stephenie Meyer's books, *New Moon* and *Eclipse*. They are slated for release in November 2009 and June 2010 and are being filmed back-to-back to keep the momentum of the first movie going and also to ensure that the Cullen vampires don't seem to age too much.

But Robert is not only focusing on his portrayal of Edward and the *Twilight* saga. Instead he has worked on other projects. One of his worries has always been getting typecast, which is why he turned to smaller productions after his turn as Cedric Diggory. He told *The London Evening Standard*, "I didn't want to get stuck in pretty, public school roles, or I knew I'd end up as some sort of caricature." (Public schools in England are the equivalent of American private schools.) Even when he thought his hair was getting too much attention in the media and had become some sort of a trademark, he decided to cut it all off. He likes to keep everyone on their toes. Most of all he wants to be taken seriously as an actor.

Another movie role he undertook before the release of *Twilight* is the part of Art in a British movie titled *How to Be*. It tells the story of a young guy who moves back in with his parents after being dumped by his girlfriend. Then he persuades a self-help guru to travel to London with him and help him rebuild his life. The director, Oliver Irving, has said that he had been auditioning for about a year before Robert walked in and that he liked his down-to-earth quality. Apparently Robert mentioned that he had been in a Harry Potter movie, but didn't say he had played a major role. Typically low-key of Robert! One of the nice things about *How to Be* is that Robert gets to play guitar and sings on three original songs, so he is able to combine his love of acting and music once again.

Robert sometimes sings under the name of Bobby Dupea, a name he took from the lead role in the Jack Nicholson movie, *Five Easy Pieces*.

Before starting the filming of *Twilight*, Robert signed up for another small production about painter Salvador Dali because it seemed interesting. It was also a movie that definitely wasn't only interested in making money and that was important to Robert too. It turned out that this production was to teach Robert a lot about how to understand a character, his motivations, all the layers that exist beneath the surface and build into the essence of someone's personality. This would all be especially useful when he grappled with understanding the complex nature of Edward Cullen.

Little Ashes, as this project was called, (after one of Salvador Dali's paintings), explored the complicated relationship between poet Federico García Lorca and Dali. At first, Pattinson was going to play Lorca but then he was asked to read for Dali and was given that part instead. Filming took place in Spain, and the majority of the cast and crew were Spanish. As Pattinson didn't speak a word of the language (he speaks schoolboy French) he spent an awful lot of time alone. And in that alone time he read everything he could about Salvador Dali—biographies, journals, looked at his artwork—until he knew everything he possibly could about him. He even analyzed a whole series of photos of Dali, working out his gestures, the positioning of his limbs, his mannerisms, and took all this knowledge onto the set with him. The filmmakers were impressed with his hard work and his attention to detail. In an interview with *The London Evening Standard* Pattinson said, "Playing Dali has been a complete turning point for me. It's the first part I've had that has required really serious thought. I became completely obsessed with Dali during the filming, and I read every biography I could get hold of." Remember, he undertook this part before he played Edward and was able to bring his experience to grapple with his understanding of *Twilight* and its world, and especially his view of Edward. He continued in his interview to say that Dali "was the most bizarre, complex man, but in the end I felt I could relate to him. He was basically incredibly shy." Just like Pattinson. This seems to be the way that Pattinson operates as an actor—he tries incredibly hard to understand his character, finds the essential key to unlocking each character, and then gives himself over completely to that character. It is a method that works very well.

At this time, Pattinson has admitted that he had a "stalker"—a woman who stood outside his apartment every day for several weeks. In the end Pattinson took her out to dinner. He told *Crème* magazine, "I just complained about everything in my life and she never came back." I'm not sure that method of dealing with obsessive fans would work now.

Check it out!

Robert Pattinson has a female West Highland terrier called Patty.

Pattinson enjoyed working on *Little Ashes* as it enabled him to reconnect with his passion for acting. He has said that he had considered giving up acting and concentrating on music, but it seems that now all such thoughts are definitely a long way behind him.

While everyone waits for Robert Pattinson's next big-screen appearance in *New Moon*, and before the rivalry between Team Edward and Team Jacob gets too intense, there are a lot of questions about Robert.

What role will he undertake after the *Twilight* saga? Will it be another big-budget production—or will he try to challenge himself artistically and find a smaller, more complex character to unravel? Will he head back to the stage ever, or would the theaters be besieged by rampaging fans?

A very important question for many of his fans seems to be whether or not he has a girlfriend. He has been linked romantically with several women, including Kristen Stewart and Nikki Reed, and he has admitted that his celebrity crush is Kristin. But they have denied that they are a couple, despite the fact that many fans would love to see an Edward and Bella relationship spring up between them. Other possible soul mates for Robert, according to his fans, include Anne Hathaway (*Princess Diaries*), Emma Watson (Hermione from *Harry Potter*), and Natalie Portman (Queen Amidala from *Star Wars*). Robert has said that he's very shy about asking girls out on a date. But he's obviously a complete romantic because he was drawn to play the part of Edward as *Twilight*, at heart, is a love story. He said in *Tu* magazine, "basing everything on love is an important message," and he also figured out that he didn't have to play the most beautiful man in the world, he just had to play "a man in love." The character of Bella was especially interesting to him as she gives up so much for love—she is willing to turn into a vampire and leave behind her parents, her life as she has known it, for Edward. And she wants to do it on her terms. For love.

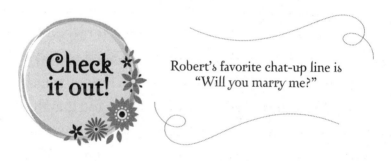

Check it out!

Robert's favorite chat-up line is "Will you marry me?"

Another big question is whether Robert Pattinson will allow fame to go to his head and change him in any way. One of the things that has stood out about him throughout his meteoric rise to fame is his friendly, down-to-earth nature. He remains surprised that anyone should be interested in him or the facts of his life. He describes himself as boring, as someone who enjoys hanging out, eating fast food, and watching movies. He doesn't like shopping, wears vintage clothes, and used to drive a secondhand car that he bought for $2000—until it fell apart. He is almost apologetic to his fans because he doesn't really know what they want from him, what he can offer them. Hopefully he won't change because people like him as he is. The way he laughs a lot when he is embarrassed, and puts himself down, and talks about his dandruff. The way he reads French poets called Baudelaire and likes the X-Men, and that the favorite girl in his life is his dog. And the way he told the *Evening Standard* when asked if he wants to be famous, "I can't see any advantage to fame. I'm happy with the life I have now. I've got the same two friends I've had since I was 12, and I can't see that changing."

So what does the future hold for Robert Pattinson? Apparently he plans to have a production company by the time he is twenty-six, as he'd like to change the way the movie industry works. He wants to take risks instead of, as he puts it, making everything generic in the hope of making money. He'd also like to write his own movie scripts and has started penning something based on his teenage diaries. And, of course, there's his music. Maybe we'll get to hear that album he wants to produce someday soon. And probably he'll be spending some time in his beloved London as soon as he can—he misses the way it smells! In the meantime, any time he wants to hang out in LA between projects he's more than welcome. But, a word to the wise, if you happen to bump into him, keep it to yourself unless you want to be mobbed—which Robert doesn't recommend.

PART THREE
Games & Quizzes

Robert Pattinson Trivia Quiz

1. What nationality is Robert?
   a. American
   b. French
   c. Canadian
   d. English

2. In which city was Robert born?
   a. Paris
   b. New York
   c. London
   d. Ontario

3. What is Robert's middle name?
   a. Edward
   b. Thomas
   c. He doesn't have one
   d. John

4. Which Chinese astrological sign was Robert born under?
   a. The Year of the Monkey
   b. The Year of the Dragon
   c. The Year of the Rat
   d. The Year of the Tiger

5. How tall is Robert?
   a. 5'7"
   b. 6'1"
   c. 5'10
   d. 6'0"

6. Who was Robert's favorite teacher at school?
   a. His Acting teacher
   b. His English teacher
   c. His French teacher
   d. His P.E. teacher

7. What grades did Robert get in his final school exams?
   a. He failed his exams
   b. 2 C's and 1 A
   c. 2 B's and 1 A
   d. 3 A's

8. What career might Robert have pursued if he had not gone into acting?
   a. A career in politics
   b. A career in modeling
   c. A career in teaching
   d. A career in banking

9. What does Robert consider to be his backup career?
   a. Modeling
   b. Artist
   c. Musician
   d. Singer

10. Robert has said one of his favorite movies is *One Flew Over the Cuckoo's Nest*. What is his other favorite?

    a. *Twilight*

    b. *It's A Wonderful Life*

    c. *The Exorcist*

    d. *Harry Potter and the Goblet of Fire*

11. What is the name of the band that Robert has performed with in London?

    a. The Shredders

    b. Blue Moon

    c. Bad Girls

    d. Local Talent Company

12. Which musical instruments does he play?

    a. Guitar, piano and drums

    b. Guitar and piano

    c. Piano and drums

    d. Saxophone and piano

13. Which actor stepped on Robert's head during the filming of *Goblet of Fire*?
    a. Daniel Radcliffe (Harry)
    b. Rupert Grint (Ron)
    c. Michael Gambon (Dumbledore)
    d. Ralph Fiennes (Voldemort)

14. What special item did Robert always like to carry around with him on the set of *Goblet of Fire*?
    a. A diary
    b. A wand
    c. A water bottle
    d. A book of poetry

15. Why did Robert almost not audition for the role of Edward Cullen?
    a. He didn't enjoy the *Twilight* books
    b. He was already signed up for a different movie and didn't have time
    c. He didn't think he was handsome enough
    d. He was terrified of vampires as a young kid

16. What is Robert's favorite kind of soda?

    a. Diet Coke

    b. Pepsi

    c. Mountain Dew

    d. Fanta

17. When did Robert learn to drive?

    a. As soon as he turned 17 (legal driving age in England)

    b. While he was filming *Twilight*

    c. He doesn't know how to drive

    d. During the filming of *Goblet of Fire*

18. How has Robert described his personal sense of style?

    a. Vintage

    b. Casual

    c. Glam

    d. Looking terrible

19. Robert has admitted to having a secret fear. What is it?

a. He hates spiders

b. He's scared of the dark

c. He can't stand the sight of blood

d. He's afraid of heights

I ♡ Robert Pattinson

British Trivia Quiz

Robert Pattinson was born in London in the United Kingdom and loves to go back there whenever he can. How much do you know about his beloved homeland?

1. Which four countries make up the United Kingdom?
    a. Norway, Sweden, Finland and England
    b. England, Scotland, France and Germany
    c. England, Ireland, Scotland and Wales
    d. Germany, Norway, Wales and England

2. What is the capital city?
    a. Manchester
    b. London
    c. Edinburgh
    d. Cambridge

3. On which continent is the United Kingdom?
   a. Asia
   b. Africa
   c. South America
   d. Europe

4. What is the name of the country's flag?
   a. Union Jack
   b. Old Stripes
   c. Jolly Roger
   d. Stars and Bars

5. What makes up a traditional English breakfast?
   a. Waffles and syrup
   b. Bacon, eggs, sausages, fried tomatoes and mushrooms
   c. Yogurt, pastries and orange juice
   d. Raisin bran cereal

6. What is unusual about driving in the UK?
   a. You drive on the left-hand side of the road
   b. No one is allowed to drive in the rain
   c. You have to be 25 years old to get your driving license
   d. You have to retake your driving test every three years

7. What is the name of the political leader of the country?
   a. The President
   b. The Prime Minister
   c. The Queen
   d. The King

8. If Robert Pattinson said he was going to "the loo" where would he go?
   a. A museum
   b. The theater
   c. The kitchen
   d. The bathroom

9. What are French fries known as in the UK?
   a. Chips
   b. Crisps
   c. Fried potatoes
   d. Twiglets

10. If Robert Pattinson told you he owned a nice flat, what would he be talking about?
    a. A pick-up truck
    b. A boat
    c. An apartment
    d. A horse

11. Which British candy is similar to the American candy "Lifesavers"?
    a. Polos
    b. Fruit Pastilles
    c. Love Hearts
    d. Smarties

12. If Robert Pattinson said he was taking the tube, what would he mean?
    a. That he was blowing his nose
    b. That he was playing on a jungle gym
    c. That he was taking the subway train
    d. That he was taking a day off work

13. Which one of these books is NOT by a British author?
    a. The *Harry Potter* series
    b. *Oliver Twist* by Charles Dickens
    c. *The Lord of the Rings* by J.R.R. Tolkien
    d. *Twilight* by Stephenie Meyer

14. If Robert Pattinson were to tell you he's "gob-smacked" what does he mean?
    a. He's been involved in a fight
    b. He's about to vomit
    c. He's stunned into silence
    d. He's very excited

Do You Know
Robert Pattinson's Secrets?

1. One thing that Robert finds very difficult to do is...
   a. stand still
   b. tell a lie
   c. fall asleep

2. Robert's secret bad habit is...
   a. drinking too much coffee
   b. staying up all night
   c. eating way too much sugar

3. Robert's secret obsession is...
   a. running in the morning
   b. collecting stamps
   c. microwaving his food

4. Robert's secret pastime is...
    a. tending to the flowers on his apartment balcony
    b. going to museums alone
    c. reading gossip about himself on the Internet

5. Robert's secret reason why he bolted out of the theater during the *Twilight* premiere is...
    a. he had to use the men's room
    b. he had an emergency phone call from his family
    c. he had a panic attack

6. Robert's secret thing he really doesn't know how to do but does anyway is...
    a. play a musical instrument
    b. drive a car
    c. paint

7. Robert's secret pet peeve is...
   a. being stared at
   b. not finding a good seat in the movie theater
   c. being served cold food at a restaurant

8. Robert's secret personal quirk is that he...
   a. can't stand watching himself on film
   b. doesn't like eating in a restaurant by himself
   c. must change his clothes six times per day

9. Robert's social networking secret is that he doesn't...
   a. get invited to parties very often
   b. know how to blog
   c. get a lot of phone calls

10. Robert's secret ambition is to...
   a. learn how to fly a plane
   b. start a production company and produce records
   c. run for political office

11. Robert's secret disappearing act is…
     a. hunching over to blend in
     b. going out the back door in restaurants
     c. wearing a wig and sunglasses

12. Robert's secret nervous habit is that he…
     a. licks his lips
     b. stammers when asked a question
     c. feels he must talk to fill gaps in conversation

Harlee Logic Puzzle

Follow the clues one by one to work out at what time Harlee and her friends arrive at school, which school subject they have first, and which fashion accessory they wear. Just use the clues for your answers.

To help you the first clue is done for you. Remember go step-by-step and think carefully and you'll be able to fill in everything. Have fun!

FRIENDS
Harlee, Luzie, Kiki ,
Marcy, Jack

SCHOOL SUBJECTS
Science, Art, PE,
English, Math

ACCESSORIES
Belt, Scarf, Bracelet,
Sunglasses, Hat

ARRIVAL TIMES
7.45, 8.15, 8.00,
7.55, 8.05

CLUES:

1. The friend who arrives at school last has art first period.
2. The friend who arrives at school first is Luzie.
3. The friend who arrives 15 minutes after Luzie wears sunglasses.
4. The friend whose first subject is art wears a bracelet.
5. Harlee has science first period and arrives at school just before the friend who wears sunglasses.
6. The friend who wears a hat arrives at school at 8.05.
7. The friend who arrives at school just before Harlee has math first period.
8. The friend who wears a belt does not have art or science first period.
9. Kiki does not wear a belt, a bracelet or a hat.
10. The friend who has art first period is female.
11. The friend who has PE first period arrives 10 minutes after the scarf wearer..

Harlee Harte is a fictitious junior at Hollywoodland High School. She is the celebrity columnist for her school's student newspaper, where she writes the column "HarteBeat."

(Over,Down,Direction)

CEDRIC(10,9,S)

CHO(2,15,N)

EDWARD(1,6,SE)

ENGLAND(10,6,SW)

GUITAR(5,13,NE)

HEARTTHROB(4,5,E)

KRISTIN(7,1,W)

LONDON(15,10,N)

MUSICIAN(14,3,S)

PATTY(6,3,W)

PIANO(15,15,NW)

POTTER(1,2,E)

RPATTZ(6,6,SW)

SHY(12,15,NE)

TWILIGHT(1,4,SE)

UNPRETENTIOUS(1,13,NE)

VAMPIRE(15,12,NW)

All About Robert Pattinson Solution

```
N  I  T  S  I  R  K  +  +  +  +  S  +  +
P  O  T  T  E  R  +  +  +  +  U  +  +
+  Y  T  T  A  P  +  +  +  O  +  +  M  +
T  +  +  +  +  +  +  I  +  +  U  +
+  W  +  H  E  A  R  T  T  H  R  O  B  S  N
E  +  I  +  +  R  +  N  E  E  +  +  +  I  O
+  D  +  L  P  +  E  +  N  R  +  +  +  C  D
+  +  W  A  I  T  +  G  +  R  I  +  +  I  N
+  +  T  A  E  G  L  +  A  C  +  P  +  A  O
+  T  +  R  R  A  H  T  +  E  +  +  M  N  L
Z  +  P  +  N  D  I  T  +  D  O  +  +  A  +
+  N  +  D  +  U  +  +  +  R  +  N  +  +  V
U  O  +  +  G  +  +  +  +  I  +  +  A  Y  +
+  H  +  +  +  +  +  +  +  C  +  +  H  I  +
+  C  +  +  +  +  +  +  +  +  S  +  +  P
```

Robert Pattinson Trivia Quiz

Answers: 1. d, 2. c, 3. b, 4. d, 5. b, 6. b, 7. c, 8. a, 9. c, 10. c
11. c, 12. b, 13. d, 14. a, 15. c, 16. a, 17. b, 18. d, 19. b.

British Trivia Quiz

Answers: 1. c, 2. b, 3. d, 4. a, 5. b, 6. a, 7. b, 8. d, 9. a, 10. c, 11. a, 12. c,
13. d, 14. c.

Harlee Logic Puzzle

ARRIVAL TIMES	VAMPIRES	SCHOOL SUBJECTS	ACCESSORIES
7.45	LUZIE	MATH	BELT
7.55	HARLEE	SCIENCE	SCARF
8.00	KIKI	ENGLISH	SUNGLASSES
8.05	JACK	PE	HAT
8.15	MARCY	ART	BRACELET

Do You Know Robert Pattinson's Secrets?

Answers: 1. b, 2. a, 3. c, 4. c, 5. c, 6. b, 7. a, 8. a, 9. c, 10. b, 11. a, 12. c.
9-12 correct: You are an insider, up close and personal with Robert!
5-8 correct: You are more than a fan, but not in the inner circle just yet!
0-4 correct: You are still behind the ropes on the red carpet, looking
from the outside in!

Who are you? Harlee, Luzie, Kiki, or Marcy?

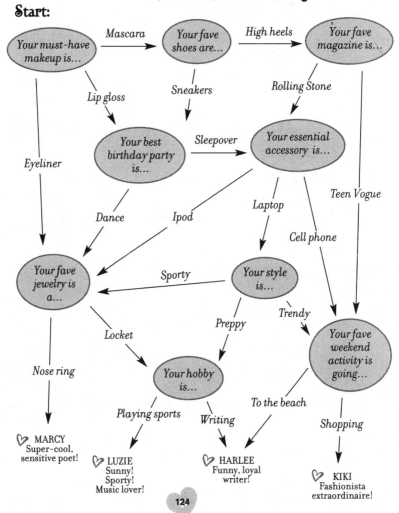

Start:

Your must-have makeup is...

— Mascara → Your fave shoes are...
— High heels → Your fave magazine is...

Lip gloss → Your best birthday party is...

Sneakers →

Rolling Stone → Your essential accessory is...

Eyeliner →

Your best birthday party is...
— Sleepover → Your essential accessory is...
— Dance →

Teen Vogue →

Your fave jewelry is a...
— Sporty ←
— Ipod →
— Laptop → Your style is...
— Cell phone →

Your essential accessory is...

Your style is...
— Preppy →
— Trendy →

Your fave weekend activity is going...

Locket → Your hobby is...

Nose ring →

Playing sports →

Writing →

To the beach →

Shopping →

♡ MARCY
Super-cool, sensitive poet!

♡ LUZIE
Sunny!
Sporty!
Music lover!

♡ HARLEE
Funny, loyal writer!

♡ KIKI
Fashionista extraordinaire!

124

CEDRIC

CHO

EDWARD

ENGLAND

GUITAR

HEARTTHROB

KRISTIN

LONDON

MUSICIAN

PATTY

PIANO

POTTER

RPATTZ

SHY

TWILIGHT

UNPRETENTIOUS

VAMPIRE

FILL IN THE BLANKS ACCORDING
TO THE CLUES (the first clue is done for you)

ARRIVAL TIMES	FRIENDS	SCHOOL SUBJECTS	ACCESSORIES
7:45			
7:55			
8:00			
8:05			
8:15		ART	

CLUES:

1. The friend who arrives at school last has art first period.
2. The friend who arrives at school first is Luzie.
3. The friend who arrives 15 minutes after Luzie wears sunglasses.
4. The friend whose first subject is art wears a bracelet.
5. Harlee has science first period and arrives at school just before the friend who wears sunglasses.
6. The friend who wears a hat arrives at school at 8.05.
7. The friend who arrives at school just before Harlee has math first period.
8. The friend who wears a belt does not have art or science first period.
9. Kiki does not wear a belt, a bracelet or a hat.
10. The friend who has art first period is female.
11. The friend who has PE first period arrives 10 minutes after the scarf wearer..